This Fruiting Body

This Fruiting Body

Caleb Parkin

Nine
Arches
Press

This Fruiting Body
Caleb Parkin

ISBN: 978-1-913437-25-1
eISBN: 978-1-913437-26-8

First published October 2021 by:

Nine Arches Press
Unit 14, Sir Frank Whittle Business Centre,
Great Central Way, Rugby.
CV21 3XH
United Kingdom

www.ninearchespress.com

Nine Arches Press is supported using public funding by Arts Council England.

For all my families

Contents

"…in the face of self-doubt, ridicule, and broader ecological crisis, we embrace our sense of our own absurdity, our uncertainty, our humor, even our perversity."

– Nicole Seymour, *Toward an Irreverent Ecocriticism*

"If anything, life is catastrophic, monstrous, nonholistic, and dislocated, not organic, coherent, or authoritative."

– Timothy Morton, *Queer Ecology*

"There will be no tidying up, dear."

– Mrs Madrigal, in *The Days of Anna Madrigal* by Armistead Maupin

Young Animal

Horniman Museum, Summer 2019

A greyhound's head, its paper-thin fur now even
thinner, wall-mounted next to a bulldog's jowl, now
static, unwobbly, and a squish-jawed (fixed) Pekingese.
The central wolf's muzzle is staged in a jaded snarl.

These dogends fan out in a ruff around this Ancient,
the great Mother, bearing all dog breeds as a crown;
their bare and shroud-skinned skulls a halo in bone,
relics of curated evolution. Before them, a little girl

weeps – just a pup. I'm here only with this notebook
and then notice her mum, exchange empathetic looks.
I move on, suddenly eye-height with *Hylobates moloch*
from Java's scorched edges. Suspended, the simian knots

of its fingers still yearn for branches. *Young Animal.*
Its gawky limbs stretch, seek the warmth and bristle
of an elder for piggybacks – to safety, the upper mantle,
and the budding tips of leaves. Now, slight and skeletal

cousin: rise from the wall, through that glass, as if
to shatter all this history. Here: I offer you my back.

If the Earth is My Mother

then the Earth yodels in carparks and stairwells. She tells endless tales
over morning tea leaves, while she gossips in customary understories.

If the Earth is my mother, she's a composer of gin and free-poured song,
a knitter of waste-wool, a forager of material, a seamstress of the surplus.

The Earth is a feeder: baker of suet islands on bubbling oceans of stew –
cook for several hundred million imagined diners. A wearer of outlandish wigs.

When Earth doesn't call, that's the worry; she gives too much away in her silences.
If the Earth is my mother, she's had IVs and pipelines fitted, right to her heart.

Earth has evolved, changed landscape. She finds it hard to rest,
even after a long and chemical winter, a malignant aftermath.

She knows her own and her neighbours' maladies, her own and others' offspring.
Earth will mother you all, if you'll let her (or even if you won't). If the Earth is

any kind of step-, -in-law, drag, foster, second, adoptive, convoluted, maddening mother
to you, then it's time you called her – right now – so she can let you know   it's serious.

garden is a dull green square edged with earth   so we reform its boundaries revise its curves rework the turf uncover the bottle-top static of plastic the crisp packet shrapnel then this pipe packed with soil which we pull at   which keeps going *have you ever had a long hair stuck down your throat half in half out the body the way you can feel the length of the oesophagus* we pull the pipe   keep pulling and it unravels somewhere under the redrawn map of this garden coiled under there an unkillable snake *have you ever had a piece of spaghetti stuck down your throat   half food half rope* and the pipe keeps coming   fills up the new round lawn twists into an elaborate roller coaster of white ribbed plastic stuffed with clay the strata to the gut of the planet   the pipe keeps untangling *have you ever had a thread stuck down your throat   as though your body was cotton and you were   unravelling* the pipe keeps going and across the fence we see the cul-de-sac sag while underneath it some underpinning is being unwarped unwefted but we keep tug-of-one-way-warring with this pipe one hand after another as it builds up around us   our heads meatballs on its unending linguine on which we pull keep tug-tugging sing a work song a heave-ho-hoist song *have you ever had a cable stuck down your throat half live half inert unconnected* and there goes the neighbourhood fraying like an ancient rug *have you ever had a pipeline stuck through your throat* there go sewer ducts water mains uncoiling under every **garden**

Dear Horticultural Mother-in-law,

Since your visit, we've continued beheading the uninvited.
We took your advice, because if there was a fifth Beatle
of the *Gardeners' Question Time* panel, then you'd be it.

The garden certainly is a fuller and more genteel green;
fewer scarlet lily beetles wage war. Though as yet, I have been
too lily-livered to execute them with my thumbnail, as you do.

Instead, I sandwich them between a flat rock and the paving slabs,
push hard through my rubber soles, until – have you noticed how
each lets out a metallic shriek, before that unequivocal crunch?

After you left, we found two of them *at it,* brazen, on the tattered leaf
they called home (and lunch and bed). How could anything
evolve to be so garish and brittle? So conspicuous

against its habitat. Have you noticed how the lily-beetles topple
theatrically from leaf to ground and then waggle their crowd of legs?
How in camouflaged cul-de-sacs, two-man households like this can

feel so suddenly uncovered? Mother-in-law, I see now it can't be Lily
-in-beetle, Beetle-with-lily, Beetle-on-lily. It's one or the other: our fond
warfare – here in this well-mannered patch of green, flecked with red.

The Radio Talks About GDP

and I imagine they are
talking about landscapes
picture Nasdaqs
as their great grey bodies
lumber across
the parched expanses
of trading floors
then thud to their knees
in cracked beds of currency

and I realise they are
talking about extinction
so in that news voice I hear
billions of figures
billions of fitful wings
as they slip from the sky
lie row upon green row
against the black screen
of tomorrow

and I remember
that each day patch-
work green chunks
are sliced out of
living Economies

How to Preserve a Fatberg

Museum of London, April 2018

Since you've decided this mass of congealed fat,
undulating wet-wipe island, Chimera of Muck
is worthy of display, you'll need to prepare
your kit, get together an A-Team crack squad
with strong stomachs and seriously
inadequate senses of smell.

Step into these waders – your saviours;
don this gas mask – and don't ask.
Descend, entering this brick-lined
Victorian id; history's gift for storing
every unwanted whim beneath
those Powder Rooms. This is the Lair
of the Fatberg, the Realm of the Reek:
everything we wish would vanish
is here – every flush and dump,
every discarded parp, each tissue
and forgotten morning after.

Perhaps you'll notice it
take a shape as its crusts grip
the masonry: a face, perhaps –
a figure. You're going to need to save
just a bit of it, or nobody will believe you;
even though every cotton-bud, every moist
wipe, every tampon, is evidence of
some body. So grip your pick-axe,
your shovel, your pen. We're going
to be here a while.

All the chipshops I have ever been to

are stacked up, a deep-fried skyscraper,
somewhere on the East Anglian coast. This tower
of bubbling fat concealed beyond Clacton-on-Sea,
Walton-on-the-Naze, casts shadows near the shibboleth of Aldeburgh.

In the blue-black-grey around Cromer's ingrown pier,
an undrownable orange buoy invites me in, to swim.

Still, enveloped food shifts across their miles of steel
counter, papers shaken through with white plastic
bollards of salt. The North Sea lingering in flesh,
mushy peas copied and pasted until no longer green.

Meanwhile, Sizewell B is a puffball on the horizon,
domed as a worm moon rising, eye with no iris.

In the steaming museum cases of the tower's counters,
the crispy sarcophagi of battered sausages, preserved
remains of Cod: body after body, dredged up in silver cages;
hundreds of Pukka Pies in their capsized foil crowns.

At Dunwich Heath, the oyster-catchers are on strike,
curlews are threatening to straighten their beaks.

The tower wavers like seaweed, shimmers – a candle,
its unknown postcode defined by the scent of
second-hand oil, slicked through wardrobes. Chips
in the toes of socks, fishbones catching at collars.

In each of those chipshops, the radio plays
the creak of a sign, rush of a wave – then static.

i swallow

my cheeks   biologist's nets
my tongue   grill of a muscle car
ten   twenty   years past
when the   base-note   bugmass
clogged our   vents
blotted   out headlights
why would I   spit out
all this nutritious life?

no   i swallow
gulp every moth
as though there were nothing else
to eat   glug every fly
green-   to blue-   to horse-
drink their bodies   monuments
in that moment

i am   not only man
on bike   but basking shark
of air   colliding with krill
lipsmack & flourish
of gill   full full   i am
not only biped   but also swift
tilt & cut   on meadows
dart & shift   for every
smaller wing than this
take all of it in   i am

not only mammal but
mechanical McDonald
this bike path my farm
ee i ee i O
the gluts of life
this sallow summer
swirls up
he i he i O
my Happy Meals

all of u   4 me   every revolution
of these legs   every turn
of this yellow Earth   is just
fuel   just protein   to burn
in my equator   to complicate
the flora   in this one
& only gut

Voice Over:
the Carrier Bag

                                    is the ghost
of a jellyfish. It stocks shelves
at all levels of sea,
emptied of its variously branded soul.
Having existed solely to carry,
now it languishes, carried by tides
and unhurried by wobbly trollies
special offers   decomposition.
The Carrier Bag may look
like a single organism, when
really it is a vague membrane   a lazy misremembering
of plankton masses.   Down here, the territorial
logos   of its former retail life   on land
fade like drowning   suns,
its catatonic handles   its eyes sunken zeros

00

The Carrier Bag   tries
to fit in with the reusable
fodder of life,   tries
                        to commit to this wafty choreography
among the weeded aisles
                        the barcoded umbra
but even in this afterlife its instinct
                            is always to   target & engulf.
The Carrier Bag   just wants to get home
               no: it wants
to unpack itself   back into this   seafloor
to become once again   bustling plankton masses

By the Writing Shed at Laugharne

"File through the flesh where no flesh decks the bones."
– Dylan Thomas, 'Light Breaks Where No Sun Shines'

A great jellyfish loiters beneath the surface:
collapsed cathedral dome of its body frayed by estuary.
Un-living water, neither fresh, nor salty, nor brackish;
water which once had fierce appetites. Now
shredding like cellophane, popped
like a dot of bubble-wrap.

Absent from this shed for months, Dylan sweated
at a makeshift office in Tehran: fired off love letters
which may or may not have been read, lost scripts
for the Anglo-Iranian Oil Company, mining the poetics
of petrochemicals. How could he know these layers of ghosts
from the ground would come back to haunt us –
a rising terror in degrees, of incremental returns to sender?

Now in the shed there's a staged desk, scraps of phoney drafts,
an aptly tattered rug. Below, the jellyfish drifts
through its flotsam afterlife, its skyward shadow
iridescent as a slick.

The Zone

"Our planet occupies what scientists sometimes call the Goldilocks
zone. Its distance from our star means it is neither too hot, nor too
cold to support liquid water – thought to be a key ingredient for life."
  – BBC Earth Website

Goldilocks
            I'll have a triple-shot polar
cap espresso in torrents
down these glacial cracks
blackening the flows
            Blondie give me a latte
Arctic with civetshit beans
swirling up from grounds
filtered through baleen teeth
            I'll have an Antarctic macchiato
a sprinkle of synthetic penguin
several sachets of brown seal
Sugar make it Goldilocks make it Love
            make the lid a tiny landscape
breathed upon by morning mouths
make it a pristine plastic expanse
a burrow hole on a drift just for me
to guzzle through where something
is sleeping Baby curled up white
whipped cream marshmallow pink
nose a frappe mammalian dream
to wake up to wake up and smell
it Goldlilocks make it make it

Ecco the Dolphin

Sega Megadrive, 1992

Ecco roves immaculate 16-bit oceans, pierces
through jellyfish sparkling their assigned scores.

Ecco rotates side on, a perpetual *loading* icon,
flips through scrolling screens of digital habitat.

Ecco is neat between the lines like practice
handwriting, before the dark ink overspills

the edges of its enclosure. Ecco breaks Tipp-Ex-
white waves on the surface with a sampled *splish*,

spirals across the TV screen, double-clicks pixelated
fish, collides, collides with muted choruses of coral.

Great-Great-Grandspider, 2120

"Love for things that are nothing like us, and which may not love us back."
– Rebecca Tamás, in *Stranger: Essays on the Human and Nonhuman*

Microhexura motivaga is my adoptive great-great-spruce-
fir-moss-grandspider: world's smallest tarantula,
thriving still, on rocky outcrops in South Appalachia

where she remains too busy for me, or humanity.

She'll never visit 22nd-century compostable cities:
messy green conglomerations of enmeshed species.
Her territory is three metres squared, and she does

not care about any sustainably developed policy;

right now, she's gracefully enveloping a springtail
half her own mass. She doesn't realise we inhaled
our bloated CO_2, learned to view mountains as

our teachers. She doesn't give two shakes of her

thorax that once you sent a passionate email
to your MP *Re: That Ancient Tree*, or buried seeds
for future nonhumanity. She is sole treasurer

of her nation of moss, constructing a funnel

8mm wide to shelter from the now customary
blizzards and rains. She jostles her spinnerets,
tethers high-tensile time from her abdomen

to the undiscovered planet of her boulder.

She is *now*: loamy water, tasted in mouthparts;
the brisk prickle of snowmelt, soaked through
this understory; the scattering of prey, away from

her clustered eyes. She couldn't care less that every

single vote was counted, mattered, because – *look!*
Here come those great-great-great-grandspiders,
those great-great-great-great – add as many *greats*

as you like – grandspiders, who'll thrive too, not caring

if we were part of the reason she's here: balanced
like (but nothing like) a world-renowned acrobat,
on the glittering white promise of her egg sac.

Terms of Service: Your Fruiting Body

after Google's Terms of Service

Welcome to MyCelium!
Thanks for choosing to mycorrhiza yourself with us.
If you're using our Services in the "United Kingdom"
please bear in mind that, as your brain begins
to be reformatted, no such national labels apply,
now you're incorporeated into our filamentous network.

Using MyCelium
You must accept any nutrients offered by the network.
Don't misuse MyCelium. For example, don't interfere
with compounds your former form is uploading.
We may suspend or stop your disintegration
if you do not comply with our hyphal tips.
In connection with your use by MyCelium,
we may send you sapling announcements
and neurogenesis messages. You may not opt out.

Your MyCelium Account
You will need a corporeal account
to use our services. To protect your
MyCelium account, keep your toxicities confidential.
You are responsible for the compounds broadcast
on or through your MyCelium account.

Your Content in Our Services
automated systems   analyse your bio-content   including toenails
to provide   tailored   downloadable features   worldwide   non-exclusive

Modifying and Terminating MyCelium Services

matter   copied   modified   distributed   any part included
open source code   made available   functionalities
        features   suspended   stopped
sorry to see you go   special   consequential   exemplary
you   limited   reasonably foreseeable
you   personal nothing   waived   affiliates   agents arising
you   losses   costs   modifications
you   should discontinue   your control

The relationship between MyCelium and "you"

you

- uploaded
- submitted
- stored
- sent
- received

you

- other
- equivalent
- information
- compounds
- content

Ode on a Black Plastic Compost Bin

after Keats, 'Ode on a Grecian Urn'

O Mucky Dalek, sat cloistered in shady hydrangea corner, I lift your lid,
your roof, your scalp, its underside covered with the squiggled pink inklings
of earthworms. Your very mind is alive! Worms levitate above shrivelled
deadheads, fur-green lemons, beetroot flashes, in your breath. Your breath!
You breathe: inhale our eggshells' brittle edges, the bittered grit of our coffee
grounds, potatoes' luminous growths, the outer hides of butternut squashes
that our finnicky intestines cannot even attempt – but you breathe all of it in.

Your appetite is grandiloquent. Gingerly, with fingertips, I lift at your hatch,
trapdoor to your lower world, where ants reimagine our teabags as hillforts;
where woodlice hurry data between them, a stock exchange of putrefaction.
Your great cylindrical belly rumbles with remaking! The fruit-flies launch
their fleets skyward, rocketed with rotting nutrients. You have become
a home for masses, a city which mulches itself back into the ground
like a delicious and urgent degrowth. Our Stout Dinner Guest, on this

garden's silver platter, we promise you the endless *amuse-bouche* of all
that transcends the plates of the louche and lavish landfill of our lives.
We will avert our flimsy noses and submit to your writhing depths.
At the allotted time, Pungent Lodger, we will draw out the gift of your
earthy laughter. We vow to witness your pastoral song in municipal waste:
Oh passionflower! Oh gladioli! I proffer my long-held longing, this love
to your ground: be giddy with butterflies! Hysterical with bees!

Tomb Sweeping Day

Taiwan, April 2020

The ophthalmologist tweezers
one of three visible Sweat Bee limbs
protruding like an extra, alien set
of lashes. Then another, and another.
In her grief, the woman hadn't rubbed her eyes
and so had kept all four *Halictidae* alive,
nourished by tear-salt, preserving her sight.

On Taiwanese TV, news stories show
close-ups on big screens, eight silver-black wings
and antennae preserved: miniscule stings
(apparently like a single hair catching fire) unused.
Reading all this from my kitchen, I can't
remember even visiting a grave –
let alone having swept one.

Winged Insects at Literary Events

I.
while the poet intones
gestures at that vital word
a translucent daddy longlegs
zigzags along the beam
of a spotlight   contained in
that diagonal column of dust
it hurtles up like a planet
swallowed by an
imploding star

II.
the interviewer offers
significant nods head tilted
at all this heightened knowledge
while a fly lands on the bookshelf
wrings its wings
fitful and ready

III.
the speaker points a laser
towards their compelling ideas
slide by slide   click by click
building cogent persuasive
in the middle of the screen
as a huge moth rests there
its wings a mystery
a tattered cloak
its whole being a comma
deleted in a thesis

Exit Only

The clock tick stutters through these seconds before men
are consumed by suits, straightening the cracked mirrors

of each other's ties. We chew pallid sandwiches, mutter
as a jumbo jet shudders the roof tiles. A face in photo

frames blots to a silhouette. Later, after that curtained conveyor-
belt, but before the breadcrumbs of the pub buffet, we stand

in car park limbo. A solitary red kite cuts the shrieking blue
above the crematorium chimney. We shield our eyes

to see this other body. Its sharp tail an arrow
away from death. We count our breaths.

Hopper Swiss Collects Waterfalls

though he doesn't want to
he tries not to he tries not to
visit them or buy them
on postcards in charity shops
loop-watch them in high-altitude
drone footage on YouTube
but still they follow him
trickles in Welsh creeks
tropical sinkholes
Niagaras Victorias Angels
white rush black blue rush
deluges through his mind
his sadness jagged glowing
blue as the frozen *Minnehaha*
Hopper doesn't want waterfalls
he doesn't want them
declaiming Kerouac at him
from corners like
a drunk uncle muttering
salespeak urgent & incessant
Sutherlands Gullfosses Tugelas
inundating his mind
like an etching by Blake
how they bore
into his foundations
cut through his granite
Skógafosses Iguazus Yosemites
eroding the partition
of his hemispheres
with their stainless steel
nakedness the ways they
cascade through themselves
from jagged precipices
into ecstatic chasms

from The Mar-a-Lago Resort Website

AMENITIES → LEARN MORE → Our steam room
was designed by legendary artist H R Giger.
Each spacious seat adorned by a womb-
like halo, while the space is kept whiter
than comfortable, its seatbelts fastening tighter
than other facilities   the artist's vision
being that every   single   guest   inside the
room experience the   soothing attrition
of a crew   whose escape pod is on a collision
course   who may have   xenomorphs
poised   in their abdomens   the decision
was recently made   that anyone who   talks
or screams   in the space   won't be heard   anyway –
We hope you have a relaxing stay.

The Channel

The BBC focus their camera on a 10-foot rubber dinghy
spilling over with 12 men and women. Thumbs-up,
hoods up – they say they're OK. From Syria, headed to Dover.

The man from the BBC points his mic at them
with its foam mask, to protect sound quality
from incursions of sea winds:

choppy out here, he says,
they're bailing out water, he says,
Coastguard informed, he says.

In my right hand, I feel that microphone's
on/off button, its plastic and steel; the foam
embrace of the lifejacket over my shoulders.

On the boat, one of the young men dips
a hand in the waves, each time the boat lifts,
at every crest. His fingertips in North Sea water:

English Channel / *La Manche* water; this water
that wouldn't know anyone's names; this water
I'll never feel, brisk and sudden, on fingertips.

Chromatophores

"…organs that are present in the skin of many cephalopods, such as squids, cuttlefish, and octopuses, which contain pigment sacs that become more visible as small radial muscles pull the sac open making the pigment expand under the skin."
— Nature.com

Across the Despatch Box

                    they make their bodies

into proclamations, pigment

                    their limbs into Pollocks

that abstract speech. They lie

                    but their skin is mainlined to

their cerebella, spots untruth

                    and scatters it like fireworks,

displays it boldly across the

                    mobile billboards of their foreheads.

Every vigorous declamation

                    and witty riposte rings only

as true as their minds permit:

                    intentions expand in stripes over hands,

fear makes their cheeks as worn-

                    green and cracked as leather benches.

The Opposition's voices force

                    them to blush in torrid technicolour.

These new palettes of their flat-

                    screen selves broadcast every doubt

or whim on patterned limbs.

                    The electorate watch these

screens on screens, peer down

                    to check what we believe,

merging with Hadean settees,

                    camouflaged and craving ink.

Minotaur at the Soft Play Centre

While the calves play, the other children-children huddle
by the counter of the snack bar (beef burger 'n' chips £3.99).
Minotaur sits on a chrome chair, latte in his vast hand,
watching the calves tumble and snort through padded rollers
or down spiral slides. He rests a hulking elbow on the holographic
tabletop and issues a hefty sigh.

Every time the calves go out of sight, the timpani of his bull's heart reverberates.
Each time they vanish behind some painted frieze of children-children
jumping, screeching, reappearing with bovine eyes widened
in overexcitement, he hears echoes of thoughts he hoped
he'd shut away. Hooved thoughts, from years within

those corridors, his meaty leaf-shaped ears rotating
like radars, shifting sharply to the sounds of those
frantic human-human feet. Soles like his
endless and disposable; heads like his
endless and disposable.

I Compare Myself to a GIF of a Dung Beetle

"There's no effort which is not beautiful – lifting a heavy stone or loving you."
 – Jeanette Winterson, *The PowerBook*

Like me, it is a roller, begins the climb diligently, furry legs pressed against its dung-ball burden, as Monday promises much.

Unlike me, it likes an all-nighter: can heft by the Milky Way and commit to its starlit labours.

Like me, its habits are misunderstood. The ancient Egyptians believed scarabs only male, their young emerging from those loaded spheres.

Unlike me, they were believed to push the sun itself across the sky, right round through the underworld, back for morning. So industrious and GIF-like.

Like me, they are various, multiplicities: Rhinoceros, Hercules, Maybug, Cockchafer.

Unlike me, their bodies are hard and shiny – though perhaps mine could be, with work.

Like me, they sometimes stop and look up, seem to wonder where the hell in this desert they are.

Unlike me, they simply push on, unconcerned with comparison, befuddled by the ethics of Egyptian theft.

Like me, they should be met on their own terms; to do their job and know that gravity will win.

Let's unite, beetles; divest our old names like *exuviae* – I'll shimmy out from *homo sapiens,* unburden myself from *man.*

Let's roll the sun together: through days trembling like antennae, iridescent; through nights like underworlds, crisp with exoskeleton.

Campers

But honeybun, we are the happy ones,
foraging in cul-de-sacs of corrugated huts,
an idyll of oinks in our neat chalet-pens.

Or perhaps space-age igloos on gridded dawns,
in spiral-tail sci-fi where there's *action!* then *cut!*
because honeybun, we are the happy ones.

We, who are over and above your legislation,
where Red Tractors patrol, windows tight shut,
through this idyll of oinks in our neat chalet-pens.

Relish these *Carry-On* grunts, our *Hi-de-hi* song.
These Rubenesque bellies coarse and hot;
because honeybun, we are the happy ones.

Our bodies kitsch li-los, adrift and mud-bronzed,
while piglets all-you-can-eat at Babs Windsor teats
in this idyll of oinks in our neat chalet-pens.

The crisp leaves crackling under charcoal suns.
Black-hooded gulls, picturesque in the glut.
And still honeybun, we are the happy ones:
an idyll in oinks from our neat chalet-pens.

Watership Down **Fugue**

"It may, finally, be in the gay man's rectum that he demolishes his own
perhaps otherwise uncontrollable identification with a murderous
judgment against him." – Leo Bersani, 'Is the Rectum a Grave?'

Long ago the Great Frith
a pink egg   the stubbly earth
El-ahrairah Prince of Rabbits
a people uncontrollable   proud
Black Rabbit of Inlé, Rabbit of Death
our long ears to the ground
bless their bottom Frith
their startail tears the hills
digger   listener   runner

> the fearsome VHS
> its dark opening
> on a wood-effect TV
> where a tombstone
> slammed shut the 1980s
> with HIV   intoned
> *Don't Die of Ignorance*

> some rabbits we'd eat
> trapped from neighbouring fields
> in a cage with a fork-shaped stick
> carrot tied to twine

> that first day in the shower
> my mind became
> the torso of another man
> my body became a burrow

a scab of sun unpicks itself
Black Rabbit of Death
visits us too
bless my bottom   bless this bottom
a tombstone on the TV
blocks the warren
this startail tears the hills
be cunning   be full of tricks

                                        other rabbits we'd keep
                                        scurry the dark alley
                                        where caged and curled
                                        was Popeye
                              pied-nipper hydraulic kicker
                                        the only one
                                whose name we remembered

                    that day Mr Daniels showed the class
                    the Durex simulator   a pristine phallus
                    some students equipped with bananas
                          others with lists of questions
                                unprotected gaps

bless all the bright bottoms, Frith
be it so   bless every startail bottom
Black Rabbit of Death
our long ears to the ground
warren blocked by a tombstone VHS
mind the thousand enemies
be cunning   be full of tricks

             white-blind rabbits
         myxied mercy executions
                in the woods where
             shivering deaf-blind
            we'd convince each other
      to grip their withered hindlegs
           swing at the nearest trunk
              like we were noble
                 don't eat those

        the dinner table "chat"
        about *specific risks*
          certain bacteria
        my blasé wave away
        still knowing nothing

Bigwig in a snare
                    be quick you'll die
rabbits fucking and dying
                        is Cowslip coming?
this rabid id
          a *Death Hole*
Bigwig still breathing
              maybe Cowslip knows?
knows the snares
            around our bodies
a tombstone on the TV

               we'd love a few rabbits
        peer down into hatches on hutches
             their never-ending incisors
                  gnawing the wire
              like machinegun fire

that day at the town hall
the blood-bank nurse folds
a screen around my body
explains how it's *insidious*
how there's nothing
useable in its veins

a warren is a scar on field-skin
rabbits tesselate   bulged eyes
our warren   destroyed
a tombstone engraved on the television
air turned bad   runs blocked with bodies
men's seismic boots   *Bigwig it's me*
bless our bright bottoms   our bodies clods
pressed together   at tunnel ends

some rabbits were just *there*
they'd run and dig
great flushed capillaries
into uncontrollable fields
bodies in elliptical orbits
bonfires of oak leaf

that day the health-worker
printed me out   my blood
suspended in the closed
tunnel of a test tube   the door
of that small-windowed room
exhaled on to a world
all corridors and risk

one rabbit   two   three
we dance and circle the sun
a swarm   *a terrible thing coming*
dusk drips from the treeline
warrens blocked   tombstone on the TV
red sun   injected into the furrows
Black Rabbit   at the verges
tombstones   toppling like dominoes

The Painted Gate

Anal sex, he says, *is*
inherently traumatic.
Then I say, and he parrots,
physiologically, as I fiddle
with the silver ring on my finger,
pick at the chair's 1970s stitching.

Picture us from above.
Notice on these regulation
green walls, a single painting:
a garden gate, subsumed
by foliage. Observe the bristle
of its thorns, the bright red
syllables among its roses.

Eight Kinds of Love

a snorkelling encounter, reimagined through rave

The eighth kind of love, as I sway around a pillar
of sea-rock, we startle at each other's floating bodies.

The seventh, when your limbs blush and your skin
sings eight-thousand synthesised octopoid loops.

The sixth, across your countless roiling ganglions,
you beckon with those extra-terrestrial extremities.

The fifth, in which our minds become tangled un-
landlocked masses of cable, meshed across decks.

The fourth, where every chromatophore bursts
upon me through Mediterranean lasers of weeds.

The third, as you throw your cloak over in beaky embrace,
I am chum for you: sliced, refracted, thrown as dice.

The second inky kind which thunderclouds oceans.
And the first kind of love, so thick and dark, it invites us

to shed our static fur, our plastic breath and recline on
this seabed dilating, with eyes that eclipse the self.

Doghouse

let the doghair gather
let it clog up vacuum filters
we'll celebrate its drifts
nurture its unruly clumps until
this whole house becomes dog
panting and hapless   it sniffs the crook
of the cul-de-sac like an unwashed crotch
its double-glazed eyes   full of sky
its roof all ears   alert to the breeze
its eaves atwitch   as the dogwood
in our garden leans in   whispers
Squirrel
from each bristling leaf
every tile aquiver

For I Will Consider Gnorma, the Asda Pride Gnome

after Christopher Smart's 'Jubilate Agno'

For her pointy hat matches her tiny rainbow flag.

For she sports a blood-red price tag of £22.

For her cheeks are flushed with the exertion
        of generations of activists.

For she is Walmart's canary.

For she wears pink and blue
        in ironic dismissal of gender binaries.

For her painted mouth is open, as if to declare that, finally,
        we are special enough to be in the Seasonal Goods section.

For the plastic compounds of her body are prehistoric.

For there are velociraptors behind her mass-produced eyes.

For she is the modern shopper's Terracotta Army.

For her bearded accomplice Gnorman
        is her partner only in corporate cosplay.

For the stubby wave of her greeting
        is about to clench into revolt.

For she is the Herald of Unquestionable Change.

For her comfy pastel loafers sprint from Shame.

For she makes cold warehouses into Pride Parades.

For she stands in solidarity with her inert comrades.

For she yearns to fight giant windmills on rockeries.

For in landfills they will backstroke with sun-blistered skin.

For they are perfect throwaway accessories.

For they propagate acceptance like desperate bees.

For it was Gnorma's queer shovel that dug our victory.

For the Gnormas have come to save you.

For the Gnormas have come to save us all.

For praise be to Gnorma.

For I am Gnorma and she is me.

Doctored-ness

estuary untouchable estuary
each every such body sneezes out bridges
lego brick cooling towers   jagged through
walkers' luminous socks
            blue and resist-
                        ant on the swollen path

water's brackish meaning
mouths over silent ridges
this bent and mottled sky
burnt matchstick trees flicked
from orbit set down in perfect lines
walkers' faces ogle in their hundreds
            they crackle on the bank
                        a nordic pole   millipede

out-of-touch estuary
wants its flesh formally
interviewed   invites diggers
untouched bed where worm
faces churn dreams of chimney implementation
walkers on the bank
                        an endless perforation

untouch touch retouch estuary
bottle flotsam correlations
neon beacons pick at this dusk
walkers backlit   anonymous interviewees
                        with their chalk membrane dogs

guttural estuary insatiable glottalstop estuary
unlit warehouse of stacked tidal printouts
walkers on hands   knees   elbows
            army crawl on bellies
                        initiate the protocol
                                    administer the remains

Spiral Shell

We, the dead, in constellations of mollusc
clutter, scattered on this grainy nethersky

of sand. For some time, we've felt agreeably
empty here, in this pearlescent afterlife,

innumerable, smattered as cheap shell-suits
or storm systems. We were the houses,

not the tenants. We were mantle-built
homes, the 3-D printed caravan masses

and unhurried seabed's gastropod traffic –
ancient as ammonite in Cambrian seas,

fresh as ragged gaps in garden leaves.
We're the gathering of moments into ages.

And we spiral, like the whorls behind
tankers, helter-skelter at ocean's edges.

We are the clarion call of the conch
in a sunrise radiant as a yellow cockle.

Now we've nowhere to go, dissolve
into particulate futures, as you crunch

across us, helixes shattered by heels,
forgetting each of us is an epic.

Unknown Distance, Moderate Difficulty

Though you might not recognise yourselves today,
head out to Sand Bay where the snow still echoes
in corners of fields, accumulating in the shadows.
As you cross the first stile, notice four bodies
you are closest to: two human males, one terrier, one
estuary – where Flat Holm reclines, Steep Holm rises.
If the brambles scratch, are you in the right shoes?
Here, the shells are held in a crescent of cheers
the smell of bubbled weeds and everything
winter washes up. Mind those jagged gaps
in the MoD fence. Stand at Sand Point's furthest extent
where the wind will not budge you an inch.
Throw your voices together, over erupting sand banks:
over your brackish months and freshwater nows
across this waving horizon, to where two bridges stitch.

Across this waving horizon to where two bridges stitch,
over your brackish months and freshwater nows –
throw your voices together, over erupting sand banks,
where the wind will not budge you. An inch
in the MoD fence stands. At Sand Point's furthest extent
winter washes up: mind those jagged gaps,
the smell of bubbled weed and everything
here. The shells are held in a crescent of cheers.
If the brambles scratch, are you in the right shoes?
Estuary, where Flat Holm reclines, Steep Holm rises –
you are closest to two human males, one terrier: one.
As you cross the first stile, notice four bodies
in corners of fields, accumulating in the shadows.
Head out to Sand Bay, where the snow still echoes –
though you might not recognise yourselves today.

Hermit Crab

fits his Saab precisely
twitches hairily at junctions
cuts up other crustaceans
his exposed capillary of torso
tattoos belted diagonally

his casing chosen after sifting
shapeshifting through forms
too dull / bulky / confined
his antennae sense left right
seek out space force space

wide claws on biceped limbs
his carapace dwindling from
electric-window extremities
to the delicate columella
of uropod on accelerator

when this shell fractures
he will peel his pallid body
from bucket seats and under
bulkhead lamps in dealership yards
form queues blanched and fleshy

In hermit crab physiology, the 'carapace' is the outer shell at the front end; the 'columella' is the central column of the snail shell onto which the crab grasps; the 'uropod' is the appendage used to grip on.

At the Outdoors Store

let's strike poses at the Outdoors Store
climb between the covers of the catalogue
have a ball where the first category is
His & Hers and we'll swap the postures
His sat demurely giggling in the tent porch
Hers foot up pioneering double-knot on a convenient rock

then let's step out from the pages
collage new ranges of
His & Hises   Hers & Herses   Theirs & Theirses
let's don waterproof boots in technicolour spots
let's slide into cagoules in macho shades of cerise
let's all deck head-to-toe in sparkly fleece

then let's go further
let's decide the category is   Tent
and we'll become breathable & temporary
we'll stride these catwalk aisles sassily flapping our vents
our collapsible carbon fibre skeletons protruding
our Velcro mouths serious & fixed

let's declare the category is   Rocks
and plonk ourselves in the corners of product shots
fabulously mossy   louche boulders *a la mode*
we'll collaborate with waterfalls in glitter & foam

let's declare the category is All the Insects Not Pictured
category is The Mountain Itself
category is The Lake Itself
category is The Ground Itself

The Ballad of the Morris *Omies*

Polari version, to the tune of *Landlord Fill the Flowing Bowl*

Now *varder* our almighty bells,
Our baldricks red, our *chemmies* white.
Behankied *fambles*! *Lallies* leap!
Flow'ry *capellas bona* bright.

We *buvare* the tankard ale,
Cold-calling ev'ry worthy inn.
Then *dizzy omies* barely know
How gyps do end, or hays begin.

We *joggering omies*, chanting songs –
Unto your *nells* our squeezebox sounds!
Oh chuck us not into a *naff rosie cod*,
But behold our *wallops*, our riotous rounds.

We're Morris *Omies*, the bones and me,
Whose *fabulosa* forries gleam!
Our *corybungus thews* do ache
The same as all who're *on the Team*.

Glossary of Morris Terms: **baldrick:** part of the Morris costume for Cotswold sides; **gyps / forries:** types of jumping dance move; **hays / rounds:** types of dance move or figures; **squeezebox:** standard folk instrument, similar to an accordion; **tankard:** ale hydration apparatus; **team:** Morris group ('on the Team' also a Polari term for 'on side', queer).

Glossary of Polari Terms (italicised in the poem): **bona**: good, well; **(the) bones**: a boyfriend / **buvare**: to drink; **capellas**: hats; **chanting**: singing; **chemmies**: shirts; **cod**: bad, poor quality; **cold calling**: going into a bar or club, looking for company; **corybungus**: bum; **dizzy**: scatter brained, absent minded; **fambles**: hands; **joggering omies**: entertainers; **lallies**: legs; **naff**: bad (from Not Available for Fucking); **nells**: ears; **omies**: friends, people; **rosie**: dustbin; **(on the) team**: someone who is gay, 'on side'; **thews**: muscles; **varder**: to look; **wallops**: dances

Witches' Knickers

"Tesco is taking a stand against "witches' knickers", the
highly evocative Irish term for plastic bags fluttering in trees."
 – *The Guardian,* August 2006

Plastikos sits on his beercrate throne
his staff of fused Evian bottles
        lids hang threaded from tattered
bright blue twine they rattle
in evermore particulate breezes

Plastikos is one with these mummified trees
their undead susurration their crunch
are his voice   his fingers extend
in bendy straws   taped to each of their ends

he hovers   drifts   plastic witch
he has embraced the crackling hex
that engulfs us
fortified his dustsheet corner
clingfilmed his crook of bramble

in what earth he can find he scratches
a self-portrait   the glyph for *man*
then the others file in   ten
adjustable-limbed action figures
who will not meet his eyes
Plastikos is the manufacturer of other
hims   witchdoctor of oily song
the vessel   the invocation
preacher of plasticity
and in this circle he proclaims

are we not just masses
of crude compression brothers

are we not become unrecyclable
vacuum-formed   moulded

may you shred into swirled masses
become indigestible palaces

reversion yourselves as
Mariana trenches adrift

in scraps brothers are we not
comingled masses   let me become

your abyssal darknesses   litter
your impurities unto me

and the bottletops jitter around them
the particulate breeze entering his
extremities   the circle disbands
as each wrings their hands and
Plastikos   is still   his face pale
as polythene   on his forehead
the pallor of glitter

Shrinking Violets

one of the Men struts through shower steam with a
WHO'S GOT SOME HAIRGEL THEN?
(hums the theme-tune from *Rocky*) one of the other Men
describes the *bird* from that party   how
HE'D LIKE A BIT OF THAT
while all this is going on i face the wall   gingerly
dry my bits   try to avoid eye contact with these Men
or these Other Men   then before i know it i start to expand

like that scene in *Big Trouble in Little China*
 – except no   not that – maybe like
Violet Beauregard in *Charlie and the Chocolate Factory*
unless that's sexist   classist   i don't know
i'm just trying to explain   find that image
but the point is   i began to expand   not in proportion
like the *50 Foot Woman*   because i'm not nor do i claim to be
or identify as   a woman   of any scale   but

i just began to fill the space   no buttons to ping
because i'm already naked except a
1980s *Wish You Were Here* beach towel
i start to become spherical disproportionate   my head
abdomen   limbs   distending outwards   but
not in a fat-shaming way   and i'm calm about this
let it happen the Other Men don't notice they're all *bantz*-ing
striking poses   don't register the slow-rising tide
of my sauna-flushed skin   my hot-air flesh-balloon

which encroaches behind them   they don't even know
because now they're comparing careers squaring up
their voices   my body keeps *Beauregarding* (if i may)
slow-mo exploding   like that scene from *Akira* the Japanese
animé film   except this isn't a comment on Japan
it's a comment on me maybe or at least these Other Men i guess

or me in relation to them   but anyway   my Cumberland
fingers start to touch the metal fixtures of the lockers
the sticky planet of my belly squidges on their backs
they turn and their eyes begin to widen   pupils eclipsed
by my unrelenting scale   my unyielding presence
my unruly second-on-second growth

Tree Triptych

Dear Men,

Is it right that we peer beneath your skin?
In summer light, your arms are curved roots

planted in the bright grass of teeming parks.
You generate energy on trendy drop-handles,

bristling and bipedal, the strands of your triceps
bracing firm and furry hands. Your fleshy trunks

heft evergreen carrier bags, grasp lovers
as if love was a real and vital fungus.

Yours Affectionately,
Trees

*

Dear Trees,

Is it wrong we objectify you this way?
Your leaves offer gruff green nothings

across dusty lanes, stamp shadows on hair-
pin roads. On prime hillside, you huddle

and creak, gesture resolutely skyward as you
rehearse at being lecterns, desks, gavels.

As your mycorrhiza disintegrates, you dig in
to cellophane diets with the tips of roots.

Yours Suspiciously,
Saplings

*

Dear Saplings,

I saw two young men – barely with shadows –
wisp along, fibres of their fingers entwined.

Oblivious to all the winters, the climates changed
before and beneath them; so many red carpets

and bloodied noses in backstory, unnoticed.
May these Saplings grow together, despite this

world of unreadable tattoos, rotted maps.
Our copse of rough bark and queer blights.

Saplings, I want so much to revel with you, for you.
But how can I when we're all in this delicate forest,

here on the brink of night?

Yours in Hope,
Men

Stubble

it wasn't my dad who taught me
the ways of razor and blade
but my first boyfriend
stood shoulders touching
hand on cheek   cheap orange Bic
with or against the soft grain
slicing through foam and fluff

my stepdad just told me off
disgusted at this new tideline
darkening the brim of the sink
how I hadn't yet learned
to leave no trace   to flush
my stubble into the mains
then moisturise with panache

*

here in suburbia we're fashionably retro
store our blunted blades
in an empty chickpea tin
wear the medals of nicks on chins

we lather our faces in natural oils
look ourselves right in the eye
in this mirror still as a perfect pool
round as a manhole cover

a barber's brush and shaving stick
instead of palmfuls of palm oil gloop
slopped down pipes   every man
drained into this same water table

Kind Words About Darkness

Into this living night, we stride
the few curving miles of hedge-
meshed lanes, reliant at first
on sight. But then, in the secret spectral
cinema of purple-black-grey
three am, away from the orange
juice deluge of streetlights –

we attune to touch, become alert
to the crunch or slop of each step, awake
to each other, the low-headed stoop
of the dog. There is space in this darkness.
A brightness. Between us and the softly
backlit branches. No traffic to face

down. No public to display to.
Not a single tree jabs at us
with censuring eyes. Just us:
our hands meshing beneath
this starlight. These hands,
scattered otherwise, beneath
the gazing windows of
a city skyline.

Instead of Smoking After Sex

we resolve instead to attack
the black mould on the walls
admirable how it's flourished
all the way up there at the cornice
or down here by the skirting
made a shadowy masterpiece
behind the picture frame
on the wall space by the pillows
nourished by night breath

its moisture clings to walls
becoming habitat
these homely taboos
how they bloom up to the ceiling
their dark droplets drip
a cumulus layer

we fetch the chemical assault
spray and wire brushes
make swirls in the greyness
but dark shapes still remain
all this moisture this excess
the supposed fidelity
of bricks and mortar
the ways bodies overflow
into other bodies
no goal but to spread to engulf

on the radio the government
struggles to control its members
viruses berth on cruise ships
continents surrender to fever dreams
this unintelligible inkblot
this discoloured room
the world has become

next morning tasting
bleach on the air
we curl into each other
tumble back into a sleep
of dark grey plumes

from beneath the pillows
it whispers itself
from behind the picture frame
its dreams billow and spore

Somewhere to Keep the Rain

after Wen-Ying Tsai's sculpture, 'Umbrella'

Today, you wake and realise
you have become a naked
umbrella; a bat with only bones
of splintering spaghetti.

A silvery second, loosed
from a severed dandelion;
stretching from this instant,
quivering. You know these days:

when you stand in the dark
silo of your senses, pointing in
more directions than the compass
dares reach. When you branch

out like coral yet to bleach,
longing for the spores to flow out
from this dark, the applause of rain
on taut skin – but flinching at every drop.

After the Section 14

'Police have banned Extinction Rebellion protests from continuing anywhere in London, as they moved in almost without warning to clear protesters who remained at the movement's camp in Trafalgar Square.'
– *The Guardian*, October 15th 2019

The morning after the news, I pass Oxford Circus where giant screens
order me to *Taste the feeling,* but when I arrive at Trafalgar Square,
all I can taste is the bitter aftermath of extortionate coffee.

All I can taste is regurgitated water, rushing from the beaks of these dolphins,
chins restrained by metal hands. All I can taste is the feeling that these tourists
are grey ghosts, that I am a ghost, on this stone grid. All I can taste is the sickly mess

in the jaws of bin-raiding wasps. The lights on police vans flashing like migraines.
The sign keeps demanding, in thousands of diodes and fast-cut swirly edits to
Taste the fucking feeling. But all I can taste are inedible scraps pecked at by pigeons.

All I can taste are three police overseeing one flip-flopped man. Then, megaphones
descend from the gritted teeth of the National Gallery; the lasso of high-vis tightens,
each jacket clutches their own hands, formal, blank-faced; eyes flit and ears await

instruction from elsewhere. By the rented Thames, Big Ben reveals its new face –
features rusted, commanding. We crowd in and nearby a cracked voice demands:
Are you affiliated? Then again: *Are you affiliated? It's a simple question.* A simple question.

Oberon Avenue

a Blackthorn Madrigal

sozzled in drizzle I amble the suburbs
seek out underthings mapgaps mess
red dash of tail – almost another foxpoem –

    across the rolling blocks of this city
    the green between moulders like mortar

in thistle nettle a hiss underfoot something
bottled hydraulic   a bodysworth of clothes
slung over branches – a dark tunnel of tent –

    across the rolling blocks of this city
    the green between moulders like mortar

Please Do Not Touch the Walrus or Sit on the Iceberg

Horniman Museum, Summer 2019

So, I clamber up, on top of the fibreglass plinth,
rise from the chevrons of the parquet floor
as though it melted into thick-cold waves

and I emerge, triumphant and substantial,
hear my epic belly boom on the fake ice,
hands slapping flatly on the hollow berg,

relaunch my fingers as weighty webbed
fins before I tackle his avuncular mass,
high-five his suedey and ample rump.

Together on our tiny island, I offer my new
form to brisk expanses, the gritty battlegrounds
of arctic beaches. My chest proud and lifted

as a dormant volcano. Then my incisors extend,
telescopic – tusks prodding at my clavicle bones.
Whiskers, these exhilarating bristles of whisker,

tickle out from the prow of my titanic mass.
We are in tandem, a double-breasted catamaran.
We are Rose and Jack on our own luxury boat.

And when staff approach with their lanyard spears,
their hunters' walkie-talkies, to stare up at the hull
of our little world, our Oscar-nominated forever,

I'll look down through blubbering eyes and briny
breathlessness, then whisper in impeccable walrus:
I'm flying.

Acknowledgements and Notes

With thanks to the editors of the following journals and magazines, where versions of some of these poems first appeared: *And Other Poems; Atrium; Butcher's Dog; Channel; Confluence; Finished Creatures; fourteen poems; Harana; iamb; Ink, Sweat and Tears; Magma; Molly Bloom; Poetry Shed; Poetry 247; The Rialto; Strix; Under the Radar; Vada.*

'garden', a poetry-film in collaboration with Marius Grose, was premiered as part of Sheaf online poetry festival in 2020 and is available on Poetry Film Live.

'How to Preserve a Fatberg' was originally written as a research poem for my MSc dissertation on Creative Writing for Therapeutic Purposes, focused on museum and gallery settings.

'All the chipshops I have ever been to' was commissioned as part of the National Poetry Competition's 40th anniversary celebrations.

'i swallow' is also a poetry-film created by Sarah Tremlett, available on Vimeo.

'By the Writing Shed at Laugharne' was originally published in Dear Dylan (Indigo Dreams, 2021)

'The Zone' is also a poetry-film in collaboration with Marius Grose, and available at Poetry Film Live.

'Great-Great-Grandspider, 2120' was written as a Bristol City Poet commission, for the launch of *The Good Ancestor* by Roman Krznaric.

'For I Will Consider Gnorma, the Asda Pride Gnome' was featured on Ben Banyard's 'Finest' blog.

A version of 'Somewhere to Keep the Rain' won the Winchester Poetry Prize in 2017 and gave its name to the winners' anthology.

'Oberon Avenue' was written for 'connections while solituding', an eco-poetry correspondence course led by kin'd & kin'd in 2020. The poem is also published in a book based on the course, *Wild Correspondings* (Elephant Press, 2021).

'Terms of Service: Your Fruiting Body' is a quasi-erasure poem, based on Google's Terms of Service and inspired by the idea of mycorrhizal fungi as the 'Wood-Wide Web'.

'Tomb-Sweeping Day' was inspired by the story of a woman in Taiwan who, "was found by doctors to have four small sweat bees living inside her eye" (BBC News, April 11th 2019).

'*from* The Mar-a-Lago Resort Website' is a deconstructed Spenserian sonnet, inspired by the design work of H R Geiger in the *Alien* films, as well as a holiday resort owned by a certain former US President.

'Chromatophores' epigraph comes from 'Cephalopod Camouflage: Cells and Organs of the Skin' by Gilmore et al. published in Nature Education and republished on nature.com.

In 'I Compare Myself to a GIF of a Dung Beetle', exuviae refers to, "the remains of an exoskeleton and related structures that are left after ecdysozoans (including insects, crustaceans and arachnids) have moulted" (Wikipedia).

'Watership Down Fugue' was written using a process of 'Lectio Divina': viewing clips from the film on loop on YouTube, responding through automatic writing, so there are fragments of the film script stitched into the work, with thanks to their originator. The epigraph is from 'Is the Rectum a Grave?' (Vol. 43, AIDS: Cultural Analysis/Cultural Activism (Winter, 1987), pp. 197-222, Pub: The MIT Press). Lord Frith is the sun, seen by the rabbits as a god. Frith has several messengers, including the Black Rabbit of Inlé, the rabbit equivalent of the grim reaper. Bigwig and Cowslip are other rabbit characters.

'Eight Kinds of Love' was inspired by a brief meeting with a real octopus, while snorkelling in Mallorca, set against some reading of scientific research where octopuses were given controlled doses of the club drug MDMA – leading to the poem's rave imagery.

'Oberon Avenue' is an actual road in Bristol.

Thanks

My thanks to the poetry ecology are extensive and entwined. I'm very glad to be part of this Great Continuum of Poets.

Poetry thanks to: Jane and Angela of Nine Arches for publishing this post-human disco; Carrie Etter, whose generosity and rigour has made me a much better poet; the Hours Group, for being our own glittery storm system.

For inspiration, learning, collaboration and friendship: Jill Abram, Rachel Allen, Miranda Lynn Barnes, Jo Bell, Fiona Benson, David Clarke, Rachael Clyne, Claire Collison, Suzannah Evans, Jinny Fisher, Tania Hershman, Rowena Knight, Katrina Naomi, Jo Nissel, Luke Palmer, Tom Sastry, Rommi Smith. (Sorry if I missed you: you're still amazing.)

To John McCullough, Samantha Walton and Nicole Seymour, for your inspiration and kind words about this book.

To Fiona Hamilton, Claire Williamson, Nigel Gibbons, Graham Hartill and the CWTP group, for nurturing a fascination with the process.

Thanks to the folks at Poetry Society, Poetry School, Cheltenham Festivals, Bristol Ideas, Literature Works, and to all my other collaborators.

Appreciation to Arts Council England's Developing Your Creative Practice funding, which made this work possible.

Thanks to my families, to whom this book is dedicated, for your various inspirations. You each deserve unique thanks, which I hope to give in time.

And to Paul, Barney and Zoot, in our verdant corner of suburbia, growing ever greener.